How to Self Publish a Book in Ten Easy Steps

A Guide for Authors Who Want to Publish Their Books for Free

Beth K. Whittenbury

KOLBURY PRESS

How to Self Publish a Book in Ten Easy Steps: A Guide for
Authors Who Want to Publish Their Books for Free

Beth K. Whittenbury

This book contains the author's opinions based on her self
publishing experiences. Nothing in this book can or should be
taken as legal or professional advice.

Paperback Edition ISBN-10: 0-09884208-6-4
Paperback Edition ISBN-13: 978-0-9884208-6-1
Kindle Edition ISBN -10: 0-9884208-7-2
Kindle Edition ISBN -13: 978-0-9884208-7-8

Library of Congress Control Number: 2016904121

Published by Kolbury Press

Printed in USA

DEDICATION

To my husband who supports all my crazy schemes.

CONTENTS

PREFACE

I wrote this book, in part, because hearing stories from fellow authors who had paid too much money to get their books published made me sad. Through personal experience, I know that you can self publish your book without actually spending a dime, and I wanted to share that knowledge with others. There are many people and service providers out there who appear to take advantage of a would-be author's desire to see his or her work published. I've known several people who have paid thousands of dollars to see their endeavors in print.

In this volume, I will let you know how to publish your book completely for free. However, I will also tell you when it might make sense to spend a little money to gain better control of the publishing process or to make your book more marketable. I'm not offering you legal advice; I'm simply giving you the benefit of my experience.

Since I also provide consulting for authors wishing to self publish their books, I have learned that step-by-step instructions provide the best help for my clients So, I've endeavored to give you very detailed instructions throughout this book. However, should you feel the need for a direct conversation with me, I can provide individualized instruction for you via the internet or in person, if necessary. Simply email me at beth@bethwhittenbury.com to ask for personalized help. I also maintain a website on which I blog helpful hints and insights into the publishing process. In fact, this book grew out of a blog series I wrote entitled: "What I Wish I'd Known Before Self Publishing My First Book." You can find that series on my website, www.bethwhittenbury.com under "blog." Just scroll down until you see a post with that title. At the end of that post, you will find a link to the first blog in that series. If you prefer to read some of the topics in this book in a shorter, less detailed format, check out that blog series.

The other reason I wrote this book is because my consulting clients asked me to write it. They find this book an invaluable resource. I hope that you will as well.

You will notice that I recommend CreateSpace throughout this book as your on-demand printer. Other on-demand printers exist and you can feel free to use them. However, I've found CreateSpace works the best for me, is the least expensive option, and has the best features for authors. Therefore, the step-by-step instructions in this book refer only to CreateSpace on-demand printing.

I hope this book helps you in your publishing endeavors. Please put out your book for the world to see. If you have taken the time to write a complete manuscript, then you clearly have important things to say. Others should have the chance to read your work.

So, without further delay, please read on and enjoy!

1 YOUR BOOK IDEA

So, you want to write a book and get it out there for people to read. That's good. Most people have something important to say. However, first you must answer an important question: do you just want to write this book for yourself and your friends or family to read, or do you want to write a commercially viable book that will sell well?

I find many people just want to write and produce a book for themselves and close friends. If so, then the title you choose and the method you use won't matter much. In fact, you can probably jump to Chapter Three. However, if you want to sell a reasonable amount of copies and maybe make some money off this book, you will need to put some dedicated thought into the project before you even start writing.

Will this be a fiction or nonfiction book? Fiction books are printed on cream-colored paper and nonfiction books on white paper. Most people don't know that, but check your own book shelves. You'll see that's the way it's done in the publishing industry.

Choosing your title is very important. You'll want to catch people's attention with your title and intrigue them enough to buy your book, if you're writing fiction. If you're writing a nonfiction book, then try to think of key words that people would search for on the internet to find your book. Put as many of those as you can in the title. Don't forget that you can add more of these search words by adding a nonfiction. You can do the same with a fiction book. For example, I named a book I published, *The Finger of God: A Young Adult Biblical Adventure*. The subtitle was actually suggested by my proofreader, and it was a good suggestion. Without the nonfiction, no one would really know the genre of the book.

I named another of my books, *A Manager's Guide to Preventing Liability for Sexual Harassment in the Workplace*. Some people told me that the title was too long. However, no matter what combination of search words a manager puts in when he or she is concerned with the subject matter, my book generally comes up first in an Amazon search, because the search words are actually in the title. This approach has earned me many sales I would not have made if my book had come up further down the list. So, spend some time thinking about who you want to target as a reader for your book and what words they would type in if they were trying to find a book like yours to read or buy. Then, fashion your title accordingly.

If you are trying to make money from your nonfiction

book, also think about possible places you might sell the book. Is this a title that museum shops would carry? Can you fashion a speech from the subject matter as a way to promote your book? Would you be comfortable talking about the subject matter of your book during interviews? Does the topic lend itself to smaller articles that could then link readers to the more in depth discussion you have in your book?

If it's fiction, is your story really long and involved enough to fill a whole book? In order to have a book large enough to put the name and title on the spine, the manuscript should be at least 125,000 words. Often, first "books" are more novellas or short stories. Writing a whole novel is quite an endeavor. I find it best to map out the story enough to make sure that you have the necessary chapter count. How to find your writer's voice, develop characters and create a viable plot are subjects for another volume. However, these are all important elements of a fiction book that can't be overlooked. Just because you are self publishing doesn't mean that the book doesn't have to be good.

Many people ask me if they self publish, does that mean that a mainstream publisher can't or won't pick up the book for their production line? Actually, several self published books recently did so well on their own that publishers then asked the authors if they could make those books part of their offerings. Those traditional publishers then helped those authors catapult to the top of best sellers lists as well as get movie rights.

One such author released his book online, chapter by

chapter, growing his audience with each installment. Then, he released the final chapter only in book form which his now hooked readers had to purchase to find out the ending. That book became a blockbuster movie last year. So, self publishing has become a way to get noticed and prove your writing is commercially viable. Self publishing no longer appears to cut off all hope of finding a home at a large publishing house.

Using a print on demand publisher, such as CreateSpace, allows you to buy your books one at a time rather than ending up with a garage full of books like you would if you went to an old-fashioned printer which will usually require a print run of at least several hundred copies. With an on-demand publisher, you can buy as few or as many books as you need usually at a price per book close to what you would receive if contracting with a full press. You can also make minor changes in between orders, so that the next person who buys your book will receive the new version, because the book isn't printed until ordered. For self publishing, I believe on-demand print is the way to go.

2 DO YOU WANT TO BE YOUR OWN PUBLISHER?

Whether or not to be listed as your own publisher is a big decision. The first thing you need to know about publishing is that every book you wish to sell to the general public needs an International Standard Book Number or ISBN. For a more in depth discussion of ISBNs, please read Chapter Three. However, the fact that you will need one for your book is the starting point for a discussion about how to self publish.

It is easier and less expensive to just use a free ISBN issued by a print on demand publisher such as CreateSpace than to purchase and register your own. However, if you take that route, CreateSpace, or the owner of whatever ISBN you use, will be forever listed as the publisher of your book. You will not have all the abilities that publishers have, such as the freedom to get a control number from the Library of Congress or to send the book out for pre-publication reviews. Although it's more work, I prefer to be my own publisher.

If you chose to be your own publisher, you can create your own imprint. An imprint is the name under which you will publish the book, such as mine, Kolbury Press. Try to come up with a creative name that is not your given name. In other words avoid names like Jane Doe Publishing. Using your own name as the imprint is a dead giveaway that you have self published the book. On-demand publishing has advanced to the point that it looks very professional. So, if you come up with a good imprint name and logo, readers will often assume that you were published by a traditional publishing house. To make sure that you will not be infringing someone else's copyright or trademark, do a quick Google search to check if anyone else is using your contemplated imprint name. If you find something close, then modify your name so that it can't be confused with any existing publishers or businesses. If you don't use your own given name, you may have to file a fictitious business name statement with your local recorder or registrar. Check the laws on fictitious business names in your state to see your local requirements in this regard. A simple Google search should answer your questions and provide the necessary forms and procedures.

If you want to run your imprint like a business and protect your personal information, you should apply for an Employer Identification Number (EIN) number through the IRS linked to your name, your business name or your imprint name. You can then use this number for all your royalty payments instead of your social security number. You can still be a sole proprietor and thus avoid any expensive incorporation fees or taxes, but you will end up filing one more form with your taxes, a schedule C. I'm not an accountant, so I can't tell you how to fill out schedule C, but it's not too hard and it will allow you to write off any expenses you make in publishing against anything you earn from your book sales. Whether or not you choose to get a separate EIN, you can set up a separate bank account to receive your royalties as well as help track your expenses and book generated income.

If all of this sounds like too much for you, just use your given name as the imprint name and use your own social security number for any payments you make or receive. In the alternative, you can just allow your on-demand printer to be listed as your publisher and still get your book to market even if with less control over distribution and pre-publication reviews. Don't let this discussion stop you from self publishing your book. If you've decided to take the easy road and just use a free ISBN from CreateSpace, then just go straight to Chapter Five and set up your CreateSpace account.

3 GETTING YOUR ISBNS

Next let's discuss why you need a International Standard Book Number (ISBN). The ISBN is a number recognized internationally to identify not only your book, but also its format and publisher. Consider the ISBN like a Social Security Number for your book. There may be many John Smiths, but credit agencies, the government, employers, etc. tell them apart by their social security numbers. Likewise, other books may have a title the same or similar to yours over the years, but no others will have your ISBN. Consequently, libraries, bookstores, google books, etc. use your ISBN to identify your specific book, as well as its format. So, if you have a paperback version and a hard cover version of your book for sale, each will need a separate ISBN.

Assigning an ISBN to your book is not a legal requirement to getting a manuscript printed. You can self publish a book without an ISBN, however, then you will only be able to sell the book privately and directly to customers yourself. Libraries will not be able to find it. Bookstores will not carry it, and Amazon can't list it for sale. So, it's best to have an ISBN assigned to your book, even if you think only family and friends will buy it. Not only does the ISBN make your book more professional, it gives it an opportunity to reach a broader audience. If you don't want to buy ISBNs, you can use a free one offered by CreateSpace as described in the last chapter.

Before 2007, ISBNs were ten digits long. After January 1, 2007, ISBNs became thirteen digits long. I guess with so many new authors writing books, they needed more digits to accommodate the production, similar to how our automobile license plate numbers keep adding digits in California. Oddly, although you will now get a thirteen digit ISBN, there will also be a ten digit version of that number. It's best to list both in the front matter of your book.

If you want to be your own publisher, use your own ISBN purchased from Bowker. Bowker is a privately owned company that distributes and catalogs all the United States ISBNs. Yes, Bowker is a monopoly. Unfortunately, there is nothing we can do about that before you get your book up for sale. So, don't buy an ISBN or a set of ISBNs from anyone or anywhere else. If you do, they will have already been assigned to someone else and that someone will end up being registered as your publisher. To be registered as the publisher of your book, you must buy your book's ISBN directly from Bowker.

To do that, you must first get a Bowker account. So, go to www.myidentifiers.com. You can go to Bowker.com, but that website will just refer you to www.myidentifiers.com eventually and probably confuse you in the meantime.

The homepage on the MyIdentifiers site might seem a bit daunting at first. Bowker would like to sell you many things. All you need here are ISBNs, so ignore the other offers and just click on the "Learn More" button in the ISBN box on the left of your screen.

Once you do, you will see more choices. Here you will need to decide how many ISBNs to purchase. The more you purchase at once the less expensive each individual number becomes. Remember you will need an ISBN for each format you will use for your book. Do you plan on a possible Kindle edition? If so, that edition will need a separate ISBN. I usually recommend that you buy ten numbers the first time. That choice gives you some flexibility and brings the price down from $125 for one number to $29.50 per number for each of the ten numbers you purchase at once. Of course, 100 ISBNs for $595 presents the best deal, but what would you do with 100 ISBNs?

You do not need to purchase ISBNs and their bar codes together. When you enter the ISBN into CreateSpace, and eventually use CreateSpace to create the cover for your book, CreateSpace will generate the bar code for you; one more reason to use and love CreateSpace.

When you go to buy your ISBN(s), Bowker will

prompt you to set up your account. Your email address will become your user name and you will have to pick a password.

Bowker will prompt you to fill out multiple pages on its site. You only need to enter information in the boxes marked with a red *. If Bowker asks you to enter your tax identification number, and you have an EIN other than your SSN, enter the EIN here. Also, on the "My Company" tab of your Bowker page, if you picked an imprint name, you can enter that in the space provided. If your EIN matches a company other than your imprint name, your company name goes in the primary space and you can add additional imprint names below your company name and then use them in your books.

If you see a place for a "SAN" on the Bowker site, just ignore it for now. If you are using CreateSpace as your on-demand publisher, all book orders will actually go through them and so you don't need a SAN which is a seven-digit number used to identify the publisher's shipping address.

To set up your book for publishing and assign an ISBN to it, click on the "My Indentifiers" tab in your Bowker account. You will then see all you identifiers in numeric order. Just start with the first blue button labeled, "Assign Title." This action brings you to the first of four pages you will need to fill in with information from your book. You do not need to fill in all the information at once. Some you may not even know until you set up your CreateSpace account. For now, you can just assign your title to an ISBN. Then you can use that number to get a Library of Congress Control Number and to set up your book on the CreateSpace site.

Once you click on that "Assign Title" button, you will land on the Title and Cover page. There you will see both the ten-digit and thirteen-digit ISBN for your title. Write those down and be careful to get the exact numbers. At this point, all you really need to fill in on this page is the title of your book. You only need to fill in the boxes on the identifier pages labeled with red asterisks. In fact, you may not yet know the answers to some of the other questions such as copyright year, page length, publication date, etc. until later. You can go back into your account to add these later. It is better to wait until you have all the information and your book is uploaded to your printer before you fill out those extra boxes.

Once you have entered the title of your book on the Title and Cover page, you can then go to the next page, "Contributors," by clicking on the blue button at the bottom of the page so labeled or by using the rectangular blue button on the left so named. Once on the Contributors page, you can add your name as the author. It will ask your first and last name on the left-hand side of the page and then ask Contributor Function on the right-hand side of the page. Mark the box labeled, "Author."

On the next page, the Format and Size page, you can choose "print" in the "Medium" drop down menu. You will probably chose "Paperback" in the "Format" drop down menu. If you plan to publish first in a Kindle or other e-book format, then choose "e-book" in the "Medium" drop-down menu and then the choice that corresponds to your Medium in the Format drop-down menu.

You must also choose a primary subject for your book. Again, you can pick a topic from the drop-down menu. If your book tells people how to do something, like this book, choose "Reference Book" as your topic.

On the last page titled "Sales and Pricing," you can fill in where you plan to sell the book, which is probably the United States. Even if you plan to eventually sell your book in other markets, you can list United States in this field as long as that country will be your primary marker. You can only enter one country in that box.

Next, you will see that Bowker has auto-filled the publisher field based on how you set up your account. If you have an additional imprint name, you can enter it in the field provided underneath the Publisher field. Until your book is published, the status will be forthcoming. If your book is for the general public, then choose "Trade" as your target audience. Chances are that you won't yet know your publication date. You can just fill in what you know at this point.

Bowker has helpful explanations of their fields accessible by clicking on the blue ? next to most fields. These will help you to understand what they expect from you with respect to each field. Just follow their instructions if you need extra help.

If you need to leave the Bowker site before you have filled in every field, just make sure that you are comfortable assigning that title to that ISBN and hit the blue "Submit" button at the bottom of the Sales and

Pricing page before you sign off. You can go back in and change most of the other information later if you wish.

To re-access your book information later, just go the the www.myidentifiers.com site again. Click on "Log In" on the upper right-hand corner of your screen. Then enter your email and password to gain access to the site. Once you are in Bowker, put your cursor over the My Account tab which lies under the Bowker header, but near the top of the page. You'll see a drop-down menu appear, then click on "Manage ISBNs" under "My Identifiers" which is the first on the list.

If you don't fill in all the fields marked with a red * the first time you assign the ISBN, don't forget to go back and fill in those fields as soon as you know the publication date of your book.

BETH K. WHITTENBURY

4 REGISTERING WITH THE LIBRARY OF CONGRESS

Once you've set up your Bowker account with a publisher imprint name, and you have a book in pre-production, you can go to the Library of Congress site and apply to get permission to request a Preassigned Control Number, or PCN, for your book. The PCN for your book lets the Library of Congress keep track of your book as well as tells other libraries where to shelve it.

According to the Library of Congress,

> The purpose of the Preassigned Control Number (PCN) program is to enable the Library of Congress to assign control numbers in advance of publication to those titles that may be added to the Library's collections. The publisher prints the control number in the book and thereby facilitates cataloging and other book processing activities. The PCN links the book to any record which the

Library of Congress, other libraries, bibliographic utilities, or book vendors may create." http://www.loc.gov/publish/pcn/about/ (Last visited March 4, 2016)

Go to http://pcn.loc.gov/pcn007.html to apply to participate in the Preassigned Control Number program of the Library of Congress. You'll see that the online form is very short. List your imprint or business name as the publisher. Where it asks for the ISBN Identifier, enter one of the ISBNs purchased from Bowker. (Refer to the last chapter for a discussion of how to buy your ISBNs and set up an account with Bowker). You can then list yourself as the Senior Officer and the Primary Contact, entering your contact information in both corresponding fields. Once you've filled in the required fields, hit the submit button at the bottom of the online form.

It took me about twenty four hours for the Library of Congress to approve my application to participate, but their site says it can take up to two weeks. So, allow some time. Once your application is approved, you will receive an email with an account number and password. You then need to use that information to log into the PCN system at http://www.loc.gov/publish/pcn/. Then, click on 'EPCN Log-in' to "complete a Preassigned Control Number Application Form for each title for which a preassigned control number is requested." See http://www.loc.gov/publish/pcn/about/process.html (Last visited March 4, 2016).

On this form, enter the title and subtitle of your book. You can leave the "Edition" line blank unless you plan to have multiple editions. For "Publisher," put your imprint name if you have one separate from your business or personal name. Since you will be using CreateSpace to print your book, you can enter the city in which you reside or do business as the U.S. City in which the book will be published and then enter the corresponding State in the next field. Those fields correspond to the address of the publisher, not the printer. You are the publisher if you've spent the money for your own ISBNs, and CreateSpace, in that case, is just the printer. Please note that what you enter here must mirror the information from your title page, so be sure that you've settled on a title and subtitle before you submit your application for a PCN.

Under "author name," follow the instructions on the form for entering your name. If you have co-authors, you can enter their full names in the spaces provided. If not, you can leave those spaces blank. Unless your book is a compilation of essays or short works by a number of different authors, for which you were the one responsible for putting them all together in book form, you can leave the boxes for listing editors blank. They are not asking here for the name of someone you may have paid to "edit" your book for you. These spaces only apply to compilation works.

Hopefully, you have finished writing the book before you submit this application and therefore know the approximate number of pages your book will have. You can guess at this number. It does not have to be precise at this stage. Unless your book will have more than one volume, you can skip the boxes attributable to volume questions.

Next you will need to list the ISBN you assigned to your book on the "MyIdentifiers" site. List the thirteen-digit version of that number in the box provided. In the box next to that, labeled "Qualifiers," state the type of medium in which you will publish the book with that ISBN, for example, "Paperback." If you know that you will also have a Kindle or electronic format of your book published, then assign an ISBN number for that in your Bowker account and enter it in box number two under "ISBNs for this title." Make sure you identify the medium for that ISBN next to the ISBN box. If you are printing your book on paper through CreateSpace, then also check the box in the "Permanent Paper" column next to the corresponding ISBN line.

Under "Other Title Information," you don't have to fill in the primary language box if your book will be printed in English. If your book is intended primarily for children or young adults, check the "yes" box next to this question. If not, then check the "no" box. Unless you intend your book to be one in a series, you can leave the rest of this section blank and move to "Administrative Information."

Here, you should enter the projected publication date. Remember this is a "Preassigned" Control Number that you are requesting. You must ask for this number prior to publishing your book. So, you will probably have to guess at the publication date. That's alright. They just ask for a month and year here. If you are at this stage, hopefully your manuscript is completed and you are just at the formatting stage now. If that is the case, then pick a month and year within a month of the date on which you fill out the PCN form. Please then work to finish the formatting and aim to get your book published within the month you select.

Enter your email address in the box provided and put your name where it asks for the person completing the form. Fill in your contact information for the rest of the questions in this section of the form. You don't need to put anything in the comments section unless you wish to do so.

Go back and double check that you have filled in all the boxes correctly. Especially double check that you have entered all the correct digits of the ISBN. You can then electronically submit the form by clicking on the "submit form" button at the bottom of the form. If you have left anything important out, the form will not submit and it will tell you that you need to correct whatever it is that didn't submit properly.

Based on the information you provide on that form, the Library staff will pre-assign a control number to each title they deem eligible. The Library of Congress (LOC) got back to me with my number within two days, but they say it can take up to two weeks. When you receive that number, print it on the back of the title page (i.e., the copyright page). Print it like this: "Library of Congress Control Number: 0000000000," only insert your number in place of this dummy number. Once your book is officially published and made available for sale, you then need to send in one copy of your book to the Library of Congress. Send the book to the following address:

US & Publisher Liaison Division
Cataloging in Publication Program
101 Independence Avenue, S.E.
Washington, D.C. 20540-4283

The LOC does not charge for pre-assigned control numbers. The only expense required is to give them a copy of your book and the shipping fees associated with sending the book to the LOC. Having this number is not required, but it does make your book appear a lot more professional. Please note that you need to apply for the PCN before you actually get your book out to the public. So, plan ahead to take advantage of this opportunity.

If you publish the book before you apply for a PCN, then your only option for getting a LOC cataloging number will be in copyrighting the book later. The LOC librarians review all books submitted for copyright, and if they decide to add your book to the LOC collections, they will then assign your book a cataloging priority. What that priority will be and whether the LOC even decides to add your book to the Library's collection is not at all assured. You will not receive any kind of notification as to whether or not your book has been chosen and prioritized, but you can check the LOC website at http://catalog.loc.gov to see if your book has been categorized. In short, it is far easier to get the control number prior to publication.

Although I'm not giving you any legal advice, I have never seen the need to go through the copyright process once I've obtained a PCN for the book. You have an automatic copyright in anything original you write. Filing your copyright with the federal copyright office costs a small fee and takes additional time. If you've gotten a PCN for your book and sent in a copy to the LOC, a federal agency (the LOC is an agency of the federal government) will have your date of publication on file as well as a record of what your wrote, because it will have a copy of your work in their collection. It would, therefore, seem to be very hard for anyone to say that your work didn't exist or that it doesn't include your content once your book is on file with the LOC. I suppose that an attorney may tell you that a filed copyright will be of more help to you if you need to assert your rights in a court of law, if it comes to that. So you can decide for yourself whether to take the extra time and expense to file your copyright. If you decide to do so, use form TX which you can find at http://copyright.gov/forms/formtx.pdf. (Last visited March 9, 2016).

If you have any difficulty accessing your PCN account after you initially set it up, the proper place to request help is through your LOC Liaison. You can find a list of liaisons, their names, e-mails and direct dial numbers at http://www.loc.gov/publish/pcn/about/liaisons.html.. The liaisons are assigned in alphabetical order according to your imprint name. So, for Kolbury Press, I use the liaison assigned to "Hc-L." I have found my liaison very helpful and responsive. When I've called, she actually answers the phone, and, when I email, she gets right back to me, assuming that I'm contacting her during regular business hours on the east coast.

Overall, the Library of Congress appears to be one arm of the US Government that actually serves its constituents in a timely and helpful manner. Don't hesitate to reach out and use the benefits afforded by this federal agency.

5 SETTING UP YOUR CREATESPACE ACCOUNT

Given all the choices of on-demand publishers, I prefer CreateSpace. You will also find that there are "vanity presses" which offer to publish your book, for you for a fee. I often find these fees exorbitant. Please avoid vanity presses. If you follow the guidance in this book you will find that there is little a vanity press can do for you that you cannot do for yourself for free. In the alternative, you can hire experts for discrete tasks, such as editing, for a much smaller fee than will be charged by a vanity press. Vanity presses may claim that they will help you with marketing. In reality, you will retain most of the responsibility for marketing whether you use a vanity press, a traditional publisher, or an on-demand publisher.

An account with CreateSpace is free to set up. There are no upfront charges for your book. You can upload edited or updated versions also free of charge. Therefore, you can write and upload your book to CreateSpace for free, and, because CreateSpace is a subsidiary of Amazon, your tome will automatically be placed for sale on Amazon once you are happy with the proof version and hit the "publish" button. So, getting your book to show on the proper Amazon lists is easier and you can more easily convert your book to a Kindle edition, if you work through CreateSpace.

In addition, CreateSpace now offers expanded distribution channels for free, meaning that book stores can find and order your book for their shelves as can libraries. Purchasers can find your book for sale on other online channels as well, such as BarnesAndNoble.com. So, I see no downside to using CreateSpace as your on-demand printer. However, as discussed in the previous chapter, I personally prefer to keep CreateSpace as my printer, not my publisher.

To set up your CreateSpace account, go to www.CreateSpace.com. When the page loads, click on the blue "sign up" button. Setting up an account literally takes just a few minutes. You will need to answer five basic questions to set up the account. You will need to pick a password. Your username will be your email address. They will ask your first and last name, your country, and what type of media you want to publish. There is a drop-down menu for this question. Click on that menu which says: "Please Choose One" and pick "Book." Then, click the "Create My Account" button. It's that easy.

Once you have set up your account, you'll be directed to the dashboard. If you exit CreateSpace, and want to come back into your account, just go to www.createspace.com and enter your email address and password. You will find yourself at the dashboard again. You will see a blue button labeled, "Add a New Title." Go ahead and click on that button. Then enter the working title for your book. Don't worry; you can change the title any time before you submit the book for review with CreateSpace. For the second question on this page, marked number 2, choose paperback.

Although it is possible to publish hardcovers through CreateSpace, it is generally cost-prohibitive and more cumbersome. Paperbacks are usually the best way to go for your first self published book.

For the third step on this page, called "Choose a Process," click on the blue button marked "Get Started" on the same line as the "Guided Option." The next page will be "Title Information." The fields from here on will be fairly self-explanatory. Here, you can enter a subtitle for your book, if you have one. A subtitle is not required, but it does allow you to add more internet search words, allowing more people to find your book when they look for your topiline. If you are the author, enter your name where it asks for primary author. You may have a contributor such as an illustrator or co-authors. If so, you can list them in the box called "Add Contributors". Use the drop-down menu from this box to identify which type of contributor you will enter. Then, click on the blue "Add" button. Chances are that you will not have any contributors, so you can just skip this step altogether.

If your book will not be part of a series and it is the first edition of the book, you can also skip the next two steps. I assume you will write your book in English, which is the language default for the CreateSpace form. If so, then you will not have to touch the language box.

Then, you will come to the publication date box. At this point, you may not know your publication date. Some authors schedule the release of their book. If you plan to do that, you can list the publication date there, and make sure to submit the book on that date. Otherwise, you can leave this box blank, and CreateSpace will supply the publication date when you approve the book for publishing. Click "Save and Continue" at the bottom of the page.

Now we come to the ISBN page. If you have opted to buy your own ISBNs as I discussed in the first chapter and described in Chapter Three, choose "Provide Your Own ISBN," the last choice in the list of four provided on this page. If you have decided to truly publish your book for free and that you don't mind CreateSpace being forever listed as the publisher of your book, then go ahead and click the bubble next to "Free CreateSpace-assigned ISBN." There are four options listed there. I don't pretend to give you legal advice about CreateSpace's different options when it comes to ISBNs and how each of them work. I would either pick theirs or supply your own. However, if you wish to know more about the other two options that CreateSpace provides and the ramifications of each, feel free to call CreateSpace and ask them. They are generally very helpful.

To reach someone at CreateSpace, click on the "Contact Support" button at the bottom of the menu which stays at the left side of your screen. Then in the box asking what you are asking, enter that you want help with book publishing and then enter "book title." For issue details, choose "Title Information/ISBN" from the drop down menu. Then you can choose to have them call you. They usually do so within a minute or two. You can also ask them a question by email if your prefer. I've found them very helpful either way, but I usually prefer to talk to a real person.

Once you have finished your ISBN page and hit the continue button, you can set up the interior of your book. This is where you pick the internal page color for your book. Remember, white is for nonfiction and cream is for fiction. Most likely your interior printing will be in black and white. You would only choose full color if this is a book in which you plan to have color pictures. If you choose full color, your books will be much more expensive to produce (almost double in most cases) and you will not have a cream background available.

You will also pick the trim size of your book here. There are quite a few choices. Think about how long your book will be. Should you choose a smaller size so that you have a longer page count? Do you want the freedom to make the type larger? If so, pick a larger size book. What size did you picture when you first conceived of your project? What do traditional publishers use for books like yours? I usually pick 6 X 9 for textbook type nonfiction, unless the book is more of a manual. Then, I cho0se a smaller size to feel like it fits in the palm of a hand. For fiction, I sometimes also go smaller, using 5 ¼ X 8, the trade paperback size. It's really up to you. Please note that CreateSpace recommends 6 X 9 for the book size.

Once you have chosen your book's trim size, CreateSpace allows you to download a Word template pre-formatted with a title page, table of contents, and chapters, etc. Basically, all the components of your book are laid out for you in the template. You literally just need to fill in each section. You can just copy from your manuscript and paste into the template, but make sure to paste into the template without prior formatting in order to retain the template formatting for your book.

To do so, copy the text in whatever way you normally would. To paste it into the template, place the cursor where you want the copied text to start. Then, go up toward the top left of your screen to the clipboard looking icon that says, "Paste" under it. Click on the little down arrow under the word, "Paste." Then click on the choice, "Paste Special." In the box that pops up, choose "unformatted text" and click the "Okay" button at the bottom of the pop-up window.

You can find the Word template for your book right under where you picked the trim size. Look for the little Word icon next to "Download a Word® Template." Make sure that you pick the formatted version of the template.

One word of caution here on the actual text of your book. Make sure to use a font that has a big "O" next to it on your font list. This type font works best when you go to upload your book to CreateSpace. The CreateSpace templates defaults to that type of Garamond 11 point font. If you want to make sure that you have less issues when you upload your interior file to CreateSpace, write your manuscript in that font and use that font for your book. It will likely save some formatting work later on.

To find out how to fill in the rest of the template besides the text of the book itself, please go to the next Chapter.

6 FORMATTING YOUR BOOK

The process of filling in the CreateSpace template is fairly straightforward. Enter your book title on the "Title" page and your name as author below the title. If you have a subtitle, enter it directly beneath the title in a font smaller than your title, but larger than your author name.

The template is laid out so that the left hand page you see on your screen will actually be a right hand page in the book. So, the title page which shows on the left in the template view will actually end up on a right facing page in the book.

The page which appears next in the template will be on the back side of the title page. It is officially called the Colophon. You've probably never heard of a colophon. Don't worry, I hadn't either. That page is also known as the Copyright Page or the Edition Notice. On the colophon, you place all that important information that has nothing to do with your story or topic such as the copyright notice, the ISBN number, your imprint, edition number, disclaimers, etc. Please look at the colophon in this book for an example of how to lay it out. The CreateSpace template gives you placeholders for the bare minimum you need to put on this page. If you add a Library of Congress number, a disclaimer and your imprint, your book will look a lot more professional.

I think it is always a good idea to add a disclaimer, especially if anything in your book could be considered professional advice, and you are writing a nonfiction book. If you are writing a work of fiction, this is where you make that statement that all characters are fictitious, and even if they seem like people you know, they aren't really, or something to that effect. I also say that no one is allowed to copy pieces of the book for any reason without prior permission and I give my email as a way for people to ask for that permission. If someone wants to write a great review of my book and quote an extremely well-written excerpt from my writing, I want them to be able to ask me for permission to so do.

Also, if you think that you will offer a Kindle or e-book edition of your book, assign the ISBN to that edition in your Bowker account, and then place that number on the Colophon as well. Make sure to specify which set of numbers goes to which edition of your book. Placing both sets of ISBNs on the one colophon will enable you to just upload the same file to Kindle as you use for your paperback book with CreateSpace. Finally, if you use CreateSpace as your on-demand printer, you can say "Printed in U.S.A." at the bottom of your colophon.

Next in the CreateSpace template, you will see a page with a space holder for a dedication. You can dedicate your book to whoever you want and for whatever reason. You don't have to put in a dedication, but most authors do.

CreateSpace next has a place for you to list your acknowledgments. You will notice a blank page between the dedication page and the acknowledgment page. This blank page allows the special pages to appear on the right hand side page of the book. Most readers expect to see those pages on the right hand side.

I've noticed that CreateSpace does not give a page for a Preface, Introduction, or Foreword. If you wish to include one of these, you can put it on the Acknowledgements page. Just make sure to change the title of the page.

If you choose to have an acknowledgement page, list anyone that helped you with the book on this page. Usually, you will have friends, family, a proofreader, possibly a content editor, maybe a muse that impacted your final book content. People love to see their names in print, so a generous list here may actually help you to sell your book later. You do not have to include either a Preface or an Acknowledgement page in your book.

The template also has a Table of Contents page all laid out for you with up to ten chapters listed. However, the template will not automatically fill in the page numbers for each chapter. You will need to add your book in to the rest of the template and then go back to manually add the page numbers once you have finished formatting the book.

I usually add in my book chapter by chapter to help preserve the formatting in the CreateSpace template. If you are cutting from one document and pasting into the template, remember to use the "Paste Special" command under the "Paste" dropdown menu on the left, under the Home tab at the top of your Word screen, as described in the last chapter. Once you click "Paste Special," chose the "unformatted text" option in the dialogue box that appears. That will allow you to paste in your text without bringing in extraneous formatting which would change or disrupt the pre-formatted template.

The template is formatted in sections, so be careful not to change the section settings, or you may find it hard to get your book looking like it should. Don't despair if that happens. You can always use the 'undo' arrow at the top of the page to get you back to where things were looking good as long as you don't save or sign off before you use the undo arrow. The undo arrow is found at the top left of your Word screen. It's a blue rounded arrow that points to the left and it undoes, in order, the last changes that you have made to the document, one change for each time you click the arrow.

You will notice that the CreateSpace template puts the title of the book as a header at the top of the left hand page of your screen and the author name at the top of the right hand side of your screen. You will need to fill these in with the right title and author name as well. Again, check the books on your shelves at home, and you will see this same format in traditionally published books.

Also note that the CreateSpace template starts the text of each chapter on a line that is not indented. That is also the way books are traditionally typeset. Sometimes, the first letter of the first word of a chapter is larger or more ornate than the rest. You can do that if you wish, but it's not necessary.

At the end of the book, you will find a place for the Author Biography. Here you can write all you want about yourself. I find it wise for future marketing to put in actual links to my other books and a link to the place on Amazon where readers can review your book.

Granted, you will have to go back and add this link in after your book is published and is up on Amazon. When that happens, just go to www.Amazon.com and type the name of your book into the search bar. When you find your book on Amazon, scroll down to the place where it says, "Customer Reviews." Click on the box marked, "Write a Review." When your computer loads that page, go to the URL line at the top and highlight the whole URL. Then, copy the URL. Go back to your book file and paste the URL right into the file after the words, "Please review this book on Amazon at:". Although, people will not be able to access the review page directly from your paperback edition, they will at least have the link to type in if they wish to do so. If you later put your book into an e-book format, the link will be there, and assuming Word automatically creates a hyperlink, already live. If the URL is blue and underlined, Word has probably already created a hyperlink for you. To check, just hold down the control button on your keypad and simultaneously click on the URL. If your computer takes you to the review page, then your link is live. If it doesn't, highlight the URL and take your cursor to the "Insert" tab at the top of your Word screen. In that tab, click on "Hyperlink." In the pop-up box, enter the entire URL in the "address" box. Then, click "OK" at the bottom of the pop up window. You will have just created a hyperlink. So, a word to the wise: do not upload your book to Kindle until you have filled in all the URLs and made sure they go to the review page when clicked on.

Once you have finished formatting the interior file for your book, go back to your CreateSpace account for your book. At the bottom of CreateSpace "Interior" page you need to pick how you will submit your interior. Choose "Upload your book file." If you follow the guidance in this book, there should be no need to pay CreateSpace to design your book for you. You can now go to the next chapter which describes how to upload your book to CreateSpace.

7 UPLOADING YOUR INTERIOR FILE

When you have your manuscript entered into the CreateSpace template, and you think you are satisfied with it, go to the "Interior" page of your book's account and click on "Upload your book." On the screen that opens, click on the blue "browse" button. This will open access to the files on your computer. Find the file with your book's interior, the one where you have saved your manuscript into the CreateSpace template, and double click on that file. That action will upload the file to CreateSpace. You will see a bar showing you the upload progress. CreateSpace is converting your Word file to a PDF. While CreateSpace works on this conversion, you will see a message that CreateSpace is formatting your book and that you can go on to the next step in setting up your book account while you wait.

Go to the next chapter now if you wish, or simply wait

for CreateSpace to finish formatting your book. Once the upload and formatting is complete, you will see a screen with a blue button called "Launch Interior Reviewer." Click on this button. CreateSpace will bring up another page with some information about your interior reviewer. Click the "Get Started" button at the bottom of that page. You will see an electronic version of how your book will look when it's printed. You will be able to turn the pages on the screen and see how each page will look when the book is printed. You can turn the pages either by clicking on the arrows at the edge of each page or by dragging the page across with your mouse from the lower corner of each page.

At this stage, CreateSpace will also tell you if there are any formatting errors you need to fix. If you've used the template well, there should be no formatting errors. If there are any formatting concerns, CreateSpace will list them in the upper right hand side of your screen.

While in the internal reviewer, check for detailed items. Does the text at the top of each page line up? Does it do so at the bottom of each page as well? Are the chapters starting on the page you wish? Are all the pages listed in the Table of Contents actually the right pages? Are headers centered? It's easy to get caught up in seeing your book almost in print and, therefore, to overlook all the little details. It is free to check and catch errors at this stage. If you find them after you've ordered a print proof copy, you will have expended money on the printing and shipping of a proof copy that isn't finished the way you wanted.

One great thing about CreateSpace is that you can upload your file as many times as you want free of charge. So, you can go back to your file, fix what you need, and upload it again without incurring any expense from CreateSpace. To upload a new version of the book, go to the interior page of your CreateSpace book account, and click on the red, underlined words, "upload a different file." This action will take you back to the screen with the blue "Browse" button again. You can then replicate the steps outlined at the beginning of this chapter.

You can upload as many different versions of your book as you want, for free, before you accept the final version for printing. Even after your first book has been printed, you can upload a new version of the book, and the next copies of your book will be printed using the latest version that you have uploaded. That fact is one of the beauties of on-demand publishing. However, if you make too many changes after your initial version has gone to print, you may, in fact, be producing a second edition which would require a separate ISBN. So, try to limit any changes after the initial printing to corrections of typographical errors or other very minor changes.

If your book is nonfiction, you may choose to start each chapter on the right hand page of the book. If your chapters did not come out that way, you can insert a page break at the end of the previous chapter in order to get the next one to start on the right hand page. If you take this step, make sure that you start from the beginning of your book and work forward. Otherwise, you may find yourself needing to delete page breaks, and sometimes they are hard to find to delete. Also, make sure that you place the page break within the same chapter section of your template, or you may create another chapter without meaning to do so.

Once you have uploaded your file to CreateSpace, you will see an option to "Skip Interior Review." If you are on your fourth or fifth upload, having just deleted an extraneous period, you may feel tempted to skip the interior review and just go ahead to get your book printed. I recommend always checking the internal reviewer after a new upload, just to make sure there are no new issues or errors that may have occurred.

When you have uploaded your interior files with no errors, both you and CreateSpace will know how many pages are actually in your book. You can then design a cover and know whether or not your page count is sufficient to generate a spine for the cover wide enough for holding your title and author name. For more on creating your cover, please see the next chapter.

8 CREATING YOUR COVER

You can spend lots of money on your cover and have a professional artist create a picture and then a graphic artist incorporate that image into a professionally designed cover. In the alternative, you can just use one of the cover templates and pictures provided by CreateSpace for free. You can also use a CreateSpace template with one of your own pictures. I don't like to spend a lot of money, so I've always found a way to use the CreateSpace template.

Besides, as you can probably tell by reading this book, I like to keep control of my creative endeavors. No matter how good a graphic designer may be, he or she can't get into my head to see the image I've envisioned. I'd rather pay nothing and get close to my vision by myself than pay a lot and still not have a final project that replicates my vision.

Of course, you may feel you have no artistic sense and

money spent on a graphic artist is money well spent. If that sounds like you, then CreateSpace offers professionals that can assist you. Packages to have CreateSpace help you with your cover start at $399. You can also search the internet or ask other author friends for suggestions of good cover designers. Watch that you get good recommendations. I've heard of many people who have overpaid for this service and then not been at all happy with the results.

If you decide to go the free, design it yourself through CreateSpace route, log in to your CreateSpace account. Click on your book title on the Dashboard. Then go to "cover" under "setup" on that page. First you'll pick matte or glossy. I usually prefer glossy, but it is totally up to you which to choose. If you are unsure, you can click on the underlined words under each choice to order a sample of each.

Then, choose "Build Your Own Cover Online" from the three options enumerated there. You'll see that the other choices include getting help from CreateSpace and uploading a cover that you have designed. Please note that, although you can design your own cover outside of the CreateSpace template, you will then have to account for the book's size and page count to make sure the spine is thick enough, and the cover itself fits and folds completely around the book. It can be done, but it's complicated and requires calculations in addition to a good working knowledge of design software. That's why I choose to use the CreateSpace cover designer, because it does all that work for me.

Once you have clicked on "Build Your Cover Online," just click on "Launch Cover Creator," you will see a dashboard with lots of choices. It will preload a default cover template. You do not have to use the one that first shows on your screen. To change templates, scroll down until the "Change Design" button appears toward the bottom of your screen. Click on this button and you can then scroll through the options for cover layouts provided by CreateSpace. Click on any of those to see how they look with your book title.

Don't worry about the picture showing on the samples. CreateSpace has lots of pictures you can use instead, or you can upload one of your own. If you are using one other than one provided by CreateSpace, please make sure that you have the right to use the image. Most pictures found on the internet are not considered to be in the public domain, so either use one you've taken yourself or that CreateSpace has provided, unless you have written permission to use someone else's picture. If you do use someone else's picture, you should give attribution for the cover image on the copyright page behind the title page of your book.

To access the CreateSpace picture gallery, click on "Front Cover Image" from the menu buttons which line the left side of your screen. Once that little window opens, then click on the "Use One of Our Images" button. You will see a "Welcome" pop up image the first time you take this step. Just click the blue underlined words, "Get Started," and you will be in the picture gallery.

You will see a list of picture categories on your left and the same list by icons on the rest of that screen. If you scroll to the very bottom of the categories list, you will see a place for you to enter search terms called "Search Image Tags." You may have to move your whole screen down to see that button. You can look through all the images by category to find the picture you want, or you may enter search terms in the "Search Image Tags" box like "writing," "books," or "keyboards," which are the terms I used when searching for a cover picture for this book.

You can try as many pictures as you want on your cover. Work on this until you pick one that makes you happy. Don't worry too much about whether the image color works with the background color of your book cover, because you can change the background color. Just go back to the screen which shows your full cover and click on the button on the left entitled, "Background Color." In the upper left-hand corner of the box that opens, you will see a little box colored in with the default color of your background. If you click on this box, you will open a color array with many different color boxes from which to choose. You can try as many as you like by just clicking on whatever color tickles your fancy. If you get too far from the original color and want to go back, you can always click on the "Restore Original Color" button that will appear next to the colored box in the background color widow once you've changed colors at least once.

Once you've decided on your background color, go to

the next button down which is the "Primary Font Color" button. Does the original default font color still look good with your new background color? If not, you can change the font color here by using the same process you used to change the background color. Do the same with the next button down, "Secondary Font Color." Work on these until you feel happy with the result.

Now, scroll up to the top of that menu on the left side of your main cover setup screen. Click on the button that says "Themes." Here you can change the actual fonts that appear on the cover design you chose by picking different themes. You don't have as many choices as you would if you were designing your own cover, but then you don't have all the formatting headaches involved in that process either. I would try all the themes available for your cover design and pick the one you like the best. You should be able to find one that suits your tastes.

Next, check that CreateSpace correctly auto-filled your title, nonfiction, and author name. If not, you can click on the corresponding buttons to correct the words that show in those parts of your cover design. We've already dealt with the front cover image, so we will now go to the button called, "Author Photo." If you've chosen a design that has a place for your author photo on the back cover, you will find this button, and you will need to upload a picture here.

If you don't have a professional headshot, I recommend you get one. I got mine done with Sean Kenney of www.bizphoto.com. I don't normally recommend services in my books, but Sean is really good at what he does, and he's really reasonable. If you are in the Los Angeles area or lucky enough to live somewhere he may be traveling for a shoot, you can use his services. He's the only person who can take a good picture of me, and he's a really nice guy with his own book out. It's always nice to support a fellow author. He was a model and actor himself before he switched to photography. He's taken the first headshots for lots of Hollywood stars. If you are sticking with the a goal of publishing for free, then ask a friend who is good at photography to take your picture for you. Please don't try and take a selfie. This picture will help sell your book . . . or not. It needs to be a good one.

To upload your author photo, click on the "Author Photo" button, and then click on the upload button in that window. You can then locate the picture on your computer and upload it into your back cover. If you really don't want an author picture on your book, and I can understand if you don't, then just click in the box next to the word "visible" in the Author Photo window. Clicking there will remove the checkmark and also remove the placeholder on the back cover for your picture.

I never used to like putting my picture on books, webpages, or business cards. Then, Sean took a great head shot of me, and I changed my mind. I now use that picture as branding. I offer a lot of different services, but my picture holds them all together and begins to create an expectation for a high level of quality of things associated with that picture.

We've become a society that largely looks for images.

I've even seen them next to my hotel room numbers, which I frankly think is going too far, especially when the picture of a pasture next to my room number does not at all accurately represent what actually lies behind my hotel room door. Some of today's images seem irrelevant. However, your picture as the author of your book is not irrelevant.

If you plan to use your book to in any way enhance your business, then you really should have an author picture on your book. If your book is your only product and you don't intend on attending any speaking engagements or doing any book signings, then it probably doesn't hurt much to leave it off. Ultimately, that decision is up to you.

Once you've finished with the Author Photo window, open the "Back Cover Text" window. If your chosen design has a place for you to write the description of your book, you will enter that description in the box you see when you open that window. Just highlight and write over the filler text, or highlight and paste in the book description if you have already typed it and saved it elsewhere. This description is very important, so work on it a bit. The book description will be a major marketing tool for your book. If people find your book on Amazon, they can read the cover. Often, purchase decisions are based solely on what that description says.

Some cover designs will have a place for you to put testimonials from others raving about your book. If the design you've chosen does not have a separate section for those reviews, you can place them in the description box along with a shorter explanation of your book.

You may also have chosen a design with a place for your publisher logo. If you have an imprint logo, you can upload and put it here. If you don't, you have the option of unchecking the "visible" box again. If you do that, the placeholder for the logo will disappear. However, adding a publisher logo will make your book look more professional, and it will look less like you've self published it.

You will likely see a placeholder for the barcode associated with your ISBN. When you upload your files to CreateSpace and actually authorize printing, CreateSpace will automatically fill that space in with a barcode that corresponds to your ISBN.

Once you are done filling in all the fields on your cover, click on the "Submit Cover" button at the bottom of your main cover page. If you want to leave that page before you've completed the cover, you can click on that button at any time. It may give you an error message if all the fields are not yet filled in and ask if you want to try again, but CreateSpace will save what you've done so far if you click that button. You can log in to CreateSpace later, go to the Cover step, and click on the blue "Edit Cover" button to pick up where you left off. You can also choose to start over from scratch if you wish.

Even if you've submitted your cover and pressed the "Complete Cover" button, CreateSpace allows you to go back in and change your cover. Again, because you are using a print on demand printer, you can make minor modifications to the cover even after the first book has been printed. However, once you've completed your cover, you can move on to the next step toward publication.

BETH K. WHITTENBURY

9 DISTRIBUTION AND PRICING

Once you have uploaded your book to CreateSpace, you can choose the retail channels for your book. In other words, you can choose where to have CreateSpace offer your book for sale. Go to the box marked "Distribute" on the left side menu of your CreateSpace page, once you have opened your book file from the main dashboard.

Choose all the distribution channels that CreateSpace will allow. If you have used a CreateSpace provided ISBN then you should be able to select all six distribution channels. If you have provided your own ISBN, then CreateSpace will not allow you to choose the last channel marked "Libraries and Academic Institutions." However, if you've followed the guidance in Chapter Four and obtianed a PCN from the Library of Congress, you will be able to market your book yourself directly to libraries and academic institutions. Direct marketing should have better results than being just one of a long list of books that libraries and academic institutions receive.

Let's discuss the distribution choices so that you know what you're selecting. First, you choose Amazon.com as a distribution channel. This choice makes your book available to consumers on Amazon. CreateSpace is a division of Amazon, and the two work well together. This relationship is another reason to choose CreateSpace as your on-demand printer. Although many people still prefer to go to a brick and mortar book store, many others are shopping for books exclusively on Amazon now. So, if you want people to find and read your book, please make it available on Amazon.

Amazon.com really applies to books sold in the United States. If you want your books available in other countries, then also select Amazon Europe as a distribution channel. Although you may not feel likely to translate your book into other languages, selecting Amazon Europe allows your book to be sold through Amazon's UK channel as well as other countries where people may speak or read English.

The next channel, CreateSpace e-store, allows you to set up a specific webpage devoted to sales of your book. The page is hosted by CreateSpace. If you click on the small underlined words, "e-store Setup," you can then fill in the blanks provided there to set up this page. Having an e-store page allows you to send people to that page to buy your book online instead of to Amazon. If people buy your book through your e-store page, you will get a larger royalty on the sale. You can also offer discount codes to purchasers of your book through the e-store.

Those discount codes will only be honored through your e-store page. In other words, you cannot control discounts through Amazon, only through your e-store.

When on the e-store setup page, note the URL to your e-store. You may wish to give people this link or place it on your webpage when you go to market your book. You may also find it useful to print the e-store URL on bookmarks or any other promotional materials you create. Be advised that any purchases made through the e-store does not count toward your Amazon best-seller or author rankings. A complete discussion of book marketing is beyond the scope of this book, but I like to throw in useful tidbits like that one where it makes sense to do so.

You will note that the sales region default choice is the US and International Sales. I see no reason to change that default unless you want to limit the distribution of your book for some personal reason.

You can upload a banner image for your e-store if you like or CreateSpace will just put a plain banner there for you. If you will send people to this e-store via a hyperlink from another website or e-store, you can fill in a "Continue Shopping URL," such as the URL of your author website or another e-store. You can also customize the text that would go along with that link. CreateSpace even allows you to customize the background color of your e-store and the text that appears on it. If you wish to restrict access to your e-store, you can make it accessible only by entering a password for people to use in the space provided.

Frankly, I see little reason to restrict people's access to your book, but perhaps you only want family and friends to be able to purchase it. If so, then do not select any channel other than the e-store, make the e-store password protected, and give the password only to those people you want to have access to your book.

You can also set up your discount codes under the e-store distribution choice on the main distribution page. To do so, click on the small underlined words, "Discount Codes" under the e-store distribution option. If you want to use one of the discount codes that CreateSpace has pre-assigned your account, click on the blue, underlined text which reads, "Discount Codes." This will bring up a list of existing discount codes. Pick one and write it down or highlight it and copy it using the copy feature on your computer. For PCs you can right-click on your mouse, as long as the mouse is over the highlighted discount code, and then scroll down the pop-up menu to select "copy." Then go back and close the discount codes tab at the top of your page, by clicking in the little "x" in the right upper corner of the tab, if you are using a PC, to get back to the page where you can assign the discount code. Type or paste the code into the box marked "Code." Then, in the next box to the right, you can choose whether you will offer dollars off or a percentage off with that particular discount code. You can switch between the two options by clicking on the down arrow next to the words "dollars off," which is the default option here. Then in the next box to the right enter how many dollars off or what percentage off you are willing to give consumers who enter that discount code.

You can have multiple discount codes for your book, all giving various amounts and types of discounts. You can cancel or change them at any time you want. This enables you to give family members one discount, friends still another and run a promotion for strangers all at the same time. It's a pretty nifty tool once you get the hang of it.

If you run out of pre-assigned codes you can ask for a new one by clicking on the blue underlined text, "click here," found in the text above the form on the discount page. Clicking here will generate a new code for you to use and take you to the list of assigned discount codes.

Once you've finished assigning your discount codes, and making note of them for future reference, make sure to click on the "Save Changes" button at the bottom of that page. You can then give those numbers to whoever you wish to have them. However, make sure they understand that they only way they will get that discount is to order the book through your e-store. The discount codes will not work on any other site. Don't let people get frustrated trying to enter them on Amazon, for instance. Such a practice will only breed bad will.

If you go back to the Channels page of your CreateSpace book account, the next channel on the list is "Bookstores and Online Retailers." Selecting this option allows bookstores and online retailers such as Barnes and Noble to order your book. I usually get significant monthly sales through this channel; however, sales made this way give you a lower royalty. Still, I believe that some royalty is better than none.

The last channel available to you if you have used your own ISBN is CreateSpace Direct. CreateSpace says that selecting this option allows small retailers to buy your book directly from CreateSpace at wholesale prices. So, please select that option. Again, unless you wish to limit access to your book, select all the distribution options available to you. Once you click on Save and Continue at the bottom of this page, you will come to the Pricing page.

On the Pricing page, you can play with the pricing of your book. Before you start entering numbers in the boxes provided on this page, go to www.Amazon.com and do a search for books like yours. Do not price your book higher than the average for other books of your type. If you are a new author without a following, you may wish to price your book below the average to attract cost-conscious buyers.

Once you've settled on a beginning price to try, enter it in the first List Price box that appears on the Pricing Page of your CreateSpace book account. You will see that CreateSpace then calculates the royalties you will receive per purchase for all the different distribution channels you have selected. You can then play with the retail price until you are happy with the royalties you will receive.

Please note that it is possible to price the book so low that you won't receive a royalty through expanded distribution. If that happens, I recommend raising the price until you get at least five cents from a sale through expanded distribution.

Also note that if you list your book for sale on Amazon, Amazon will likely discount the price. However, the royalty you establish through the CreateSpace pricing page will not change. In other words, Amazon eats the amount of the discount. So, the only way that discount negatively affects you is that it will be hard for you to sell the book yourself for more than people can buy it for on Amazon. However, remember that Amazon also tacks on shipping and taxes, so unless you're selling to an Amazon Prime member and won't pay the sales tax yourself, you may still have a price advantage over even a discounted Amazon sale.

Below that first box on the Pricing Page are other boxes that allow you to set different prices for different geographical areas. Above those bigger boxes is a little box with the words, "Yes, suggest a price based on U.S. price." Basically, CreateSpace is offering to do the exchange rate calculation for you. I usually take them up on this offer and check this little box for each separate currency listed on the pricing page. Make sure to save your pricing choices before leaving this page.

Next, you will see the option for the "Description" page. Click on this option from the menu on the left side of the CreateSpace screen. Here you have the option to enter up to a 4000 character description of your book. Take advantage of this opportunity to put key word search terms into your book description. I often use the same description I place on the back cover of my book. However, CreateSpace allows you more characters for your book description than for the brief description that will fit on you back cover. So, if you wish to expand the description that will show on your e-store page, go ahead and write more in this description box if you want.

Below the big box for the book description, you'll see a place to enter a Bool Industry Standards and Communications (BISAC) category. BISAC categories are used by book-sellers to aid in identifying books by their subject matter. There are official BISAC codes, and CreateSpace gives you a place to enter a code if you have one. If not, then just go ahead and choose your category from the drop-down menu provided there by CreateSpace. To access that menu, just click on the blue "Choose . . ." button next to the BISAC box provided on the "Description" page. First, choose from a category on the left, and then choose a corresponding category from the list on the right. For this book, I chose, "Reference/Handbooks & Manuals."

Under the part of the page labeled "Additional Information," you can add an author bio by clicking on the corresponding button and then typing in up to 2500 characters in the box that appears. You book language will probably be English and the "Country of Publication" should be that in which you bought your ISBN. If you used a CreateSpace provided ISBN or bought your ISBN from Bowker, your country of publication is the United States.

Last, you can list up to five search words that will help those seeking a book like yours online to find your book. Separate each search word or phrase with a comma. If your book contains "Adult" (meaning basically erotica) content, check that box. Click the large-print box only if you are offering this edition of your book in larger than normal print designed for those with eyesight challenges.

Then, click on the "Save and Continue" button. That action will bring you to the Kindle publication page. If you wish to publish your book on Kindle, you can follow the instructions there. I usually wait until I have my paperback edition published and for sale before I also list my book for sale as a Kindle edition.

Once you have finished the nine steps previously described, your book is ready for file review.

10 PRESSING THE "PUBLISH" BUTTON

If you've followed all the steps outlined in the previous chapters, you should see a check mark beside all the items listed under "Set Up" category on the left side of your CreateSpace book account screen. If you're not already on the "Complete Setup" screen, simply click on those words under the "Set Up" category on your left-hand menu. Here you have one more opportunity to edit the title and major set up features of your book. If you are satisfied with those listed there, you can go to the bottom of the page and click on "Submit Files for Review."

Clicking on that button will cause CreateSpace to check all your files, including your cover file, for compliance with the CreateSpace PDF submission requirements. If you have used the CreateSpace template, checked the interior reviewer to see that there are no errors with that part of the file, and used the CreateSpace cover creator, your files should meet the CreateSpace PDF submission requirements. However, you'll need to wait about twenty-four hours for an email from CreateSpace letting you know that you have passed their inspection.

You will note that CreateSpace recommends for you to work on your distribution options while you wait to hear from them. If you've followed the instructions in the book, you've already done that, but you can take the time now to go back and fill in some places like the book description in your e-store if you didn't do that the first time around. If you delayed following the advice in chapter nine of this book, you can also go back and take those steps now.

If you press the "Submit Files for Review" button, you are acquiescing to the CreateSpace "Membership Agreement." You can read the agreement by clicking on those underlined words. Although you can't negotiate this agreement, it's always a good idea to know what you are, in effect, signing by clicking on the submit button.

After CreateSpace completes the file review, you can order a proof copy of your book, or you can use one of the digital proof option given by CreateSpace. The digital proof option allows you to look at your book on the computer screen. Although this version will be laid out just like your printed book, it may not be the same size as your actual book will be when printed by CreateSpace. I would recommend you pay for an actual hard copy proof of your book to be sent to you by CreateSpace and read it carefully, looking for any errors. No matter how closely you checked the internal reviewer version, things look very different in print than they do on the computer screen.

Once you've received your proof copy, reviewed it, and decided that you're thrilled with the book, go ahead and approve your proof by clicking on the blue "Approve" button in the "Approve Proof" box on the "Proof Your Book" page under the "Review" menu item on the left of your CreateSpace book screen. CreateSpace will then ask you to confirm your approval. You can still make changes after you approve your proof and your book has been published. You will have to go through the review process again, but you can make changes to the interior. However, you cannot change the trim size, interior color, or ISBN after you approve the proof and therefore, publish your book. You can make changes to the cover finish, pricing, and description of your book at any time without regenerating the review process. Please be aware that if you make changes and upload a new interior file, your book will not be for sale through CreateSpace while your new file is being reviewed.

Once you've approved your proof, you have published your book! Your book will show as available on Amazon.com within three to five business days; however, CreateSpace will make it instantly available in your e-store. CreateSpace will give you the URL to your store on the "Proof Your Book" page of the "Review" menu in your CreateSpace book account. Write down this URL and proudly send it to your friends and family, letting them know that your book is available for sale there and should show on Amazon shortly. Then, you can click on "Marketing Center" to see some helpful guidance from CreateSpace. If you wish to also publish a Kindle edition of your book, please see Appendix A.

Congratulations! You've published your book. I wish you many happy sales and a real sense of accomplishment!

Appendix A – Publishing a Kindle Edition

If you want to also publish a Kindle edition of your book, you can click on the "Distribute" option on the CreateSpace book account menu. Then, choose the last option under Distribute, "Publish on Kindle." On the next page that appears, click on and fill in the bubbles next to "This is not a public domain work" and "Enable digital rights management." Then, click on the "Submit files to KDP" button.

Once on the Kindle set up page, you must decide if you wish to enroll your book in KDP Select. Doing so has several benefits which Amazon explains on that page. However, if you enroll in KDP Select, you must not offer your book for sale in a digital medium anywhere else such as BarnesandNoble.com. You can un-enroll from KDP Select after ninety days, if you decide you want to pursue other digital vendors at that time. If you agree to enroll in KDP Select, click on the box next to "Enroll this book in KDP Select."

You should find your book title automatically entered. However, if you have a subtitle, you will need to enter it in the box provided. Place your imprint name in the "Publisher" box, if you have one. You can also add your book description in the box provided. You will next see a ISBN (optional) box. There, place your ISBN assigned to the ebook version of your book if you are acting as your own publisher. Make sure you are using the ISBN assigned to your ebook version and NOT the ISBN assigned to the print version of your book. If you used a free CreateSpace generated ISBN for your hard copy book, you can leave this box blank.

Verify your publishing rights by clicking on the bubble next to "This is not a public domain work and I hold the necessary publishing rights." Then, pick the best two categories which describe your book under the heading, "Target Your Book to Customers." If you have a children's book, you can fill in the age and grade appropriate questions. If not, just leave them blank.

If you have already published the print version of your book, go ahead and choose the "I am ready to release this book now" option. If you've followed the instructions in this book, you should be able to publish the same interior file and cover you used for your paperback as a Kindle edition. You should see those files already loaded on the Kindle set up page. CreateSpace will do the necessary Kindle formatting for you for free. Make sure that they say there are no spelling errors and that the upload and conversion was successful.

Next, be sure to preview the Kindle edition digitally before approving publication of that edition. You may see that you need to go back and fix some formatting in your interior file, and then try it again by uploading the new file through your CreateSpace account. Sometimes, no matter how much you tweak your interior files, your text will not load the same way on a Kindle device as it does on a printed page. Don't be discouraged. Since digital devices may be rotated between portrait and landscape, the pages may cut off in places you don't intend.

When you have completed the actions items on that page, click "Save and Continue." Next, make sure that "worldwide rights" is checked. Then, you can decide on your royalty. If you have chosen to enroll the book in KDP Select, you'll have an option of obtaining a seventy percent royalty. If so, then click on that option. Kindle explains the royalty options along the side of that page and also if you click on the blue "What's this" type next to the royalty options. Then, you can choose a price for your Kindle edition.

Next, decide if you would like to allow your book to be placed in the MatchBook program and, if so, for what price. Basically, you will be allowing those who purchased your print book to receive a discount when they additionally purchase your Kindle edition. You can also decide if you want to allow Kindle purchasers to lend your book to others.

At the bottom of the page, you will need to click on the box agreeing to Kindle's terms and conditions, before you actually can publish a Kindle edition. If you are waiting for a new version of your interior file to load, click "Save Draft" at the bottom of the page. You will be able to come back later to actually publish the Kindle edition.

When you are happy with the version showing in the Kindle reviewer, you can click on "Save and Publish." Once you've approved the Kindle file and saved all the information, your book will be available for sale in two types of editions. Congratulations! You will be off to a great start.

ACKNOWLEDGEMENTS

The author wishes to thank John and William Whittenbury for proof reading this book. She also wishes to thank fellow author, Vickey Kall, who encourages fellow writers. She is herself a great writer of several wonderful books. Please check out her works on Amazon.

Special thanks to my cousin, Barbara Hunter, whose project, turning family history into a readable and publishable paperback with my help, inspired me to finally sit down and write this book. Also, thanks to my wonderful consulting client, Cathy Magruder, whose precious children's picture book, *When Henry Met Santa Claus*, also inspired me to put my advice in writing for others to read.

Thanks to you all!

ABOUT THE AUTHOR

Beth K. Whittenbury writes on a variety of topics and consults with authors wishing to self publish their works. She can be reached through her website, www.bethwhittenbury.com or via email to beth@bethwhittenbury.com

Please review this book on Amazon at https://www.amazon.com/review/create-review?ie=UTF8&asin=0988420861&channel=detail-glance&nodeID=283155&ref_=cm_cr_dp_no_rvw_e&store=books#

Other books by Beth K. Whittenbury:

A Manager's Guide to Preventing Sexual Harassment in the Workplace

Investigating the Workplace Harassment Claim

Just Love Him, I Guess (Children's Picture Book)

Also published by Kolbury Press:

The Finger of God: A Young Adult Biblical Adventure

CPSIA information can be obtained
at www.ICGtesting.com
Printed in the USA
FSOW03n1050250716
23087FS